WHOSE CH IS IT ANYWAY?

An alternative Church Warden's Guide to Appointing a Minister

Edited by Hugh Balfour

PUBLISHED BY THE GOOD BOOK COMPANY FOR

Reform

Whose church is it anyway?
© Reform/The Good Book Company 2001
ISBN: 1-873166-31-1

The Good Book Company
Elm House, 37 Elm Road,
New Malden, Surrey KT3 3HB
Tel: 020-8942-0880
Fax: 020-8942-0990
e-mail: Admin@thegoodbook.co.uk
www.thegoodbook.co.uk

Reform
c/o Christ Church, Fulwood,
Canterbury Avenue,
Sheffield S10 3RT,
Tel: 0114 230 1911
Fax: 0114 230 6568

Chapter 6: Who pastors your Pastor? is abridged
from *Fellow Workers* © St Matthias Press 1992

CONTENTS

Foreword

During the last thirty years, radical changes have occurred in the Church of England. A dual process of centralisation and a vast expansion of the Church's bureaucracy have gone on apace.

First, we have seen bishops seeking much greater control over local churches in areas such as the appointment of clergy. With regard to curates, the bishop has almost complete control over which parishes may have assistant ordained staff. Centrally, the Commission chaired by Michael Turnbull, the Bishop of Durham, on the organisation of the Church of England, has, among other things, recommended the creation of an Archbishops' Council to make major policy decisions for General Synod to pass. This might indeed streamline the church administratively, but would concentrate huge power in the hands of fifteen or twenty people.

Secondly, since its inception in 1970 the General Synod has spawned a network of boards and committees, each with at their supporting bureaucracy. These have, in part at least, been replicated at diocesan level. At the same time the number of church "dignitaries" (assistant bishops, archdeacons etc) dramatically increased, while the number of parochial clergy has steadily declined. So in 1961 there were 12,886 clergy and 231 dignitaries. But by 1991 there were 9,671 clergy and 385 dignitaries: a 25% reduction in parochial clergy, and a 66% increase in dignitaries!

These two processes of centralising power and an expanding bureaucracy are the result of two different sets of pressures. First there are the external pressures. This is only what is going on in the rest of society. Note the huge centralisation of political power to Westminster since 1979, and the invasion of petty bureaucracy into almost every area of life.

But secondly, and more significantly, there is the malign influence of liberal theology which has taken root in almost every part of the church. Traditionally the glue which held together the Anglican Church in this country was the basic Christian doctrines, taken from the Scriptures, which are set out in the Creeds, the Thirty-Nine Articles and the Book of Common Prayer. As liberalism has advanced, and one by one fundamental doctrines have been denied, so the old glue of doctrine has lost its power. Centralisation becomes the new glue and its theological rationalisation is the slogan "the bishop is the focus of unity". Thus, today, a clergyman is allowed to challenge any point of theological orthodoxy unopposed, but is promptly accused of disloyalty if he challenges the bureacracy. The Church has moved from being a spiritual organisation to being a bureaucratic one.

The result is that bishops and archdeacons are increasingly becoming managers. Moreover, they are managers of an institution which is in a slow but inexorable decline. This means that they become expert at managing decline, but find growth rather harder to handle. This management model of church leadership means, for example that it is very difficult for them to approach matters of finance with real faith, and plan for growth when the money isn't there, trusting God to provide. That is not how sensible management works!

This may all seem rather remote and irrelevant to everyday life in your local church. At one level it is—until you come to appoint a new vicar. Then if you are unfamiliar with the appointment procedures, or if you do not know what questions to ask a candidate, or do not have a clear idea of what sort of ministry you need, you are vulnerable. Diocesan officials may try and manipulate you to extend the interregnum, or foist their preferred candidate upon you, or amalgamate your church into a team ministry. All these things have been tried on churches, with varying degrees of success.

Such pressures mean that we cannot assume that evangelical ministry will automatically continue. That is the reason for this book. My hope and prayer is that it will prepare you for the vital task of appointing a new leader for your church when the occasion arises. Choosing a new vicar is the most important task that any lay church leader will ever undertake. Your decision will affect the nature and effectiveness of your church for years to come. The purpose of this book is, by God's grace, to help you get that decision right.

We want to make it clear that this book is principally about the appointment of incumbents and not assistant staff, although there will be many principles that apply to both. Because of Reform's position on the ordination of women, we have assumed throughout that the incumbent will be a man.

Hugh Balfour, January 1997

So who does your church belong to? Who is in charge? There are many answers to that question. The people, the vicar, the churchwardens, the bishops, the trustees, the Church of England: all would seem to have some kind of varying authority over the local congregation. Where people are unclear or uncertain about their privilege and responsibility in church leadership, the way is left open to those who may have different ideas about what should go on in the life of your congregation.

CHAPTER 1

Whose church is it anyway?

RIGHT ANSWERS AND HELPFUL ANSWERS

The question "Whose church is it anyway?" has only one possible answer: "God's church". Unfortunately, this is one of those cases where the right answer fails to help our understanding, since Christians of every persuasion, from traditionalist Catholic to charismatic Quaker, would agree that it is God's church, while disagreeing radically about how that plays out in practice. To be helpful our answer must enable us to distinguish right approaches to church from wrong ones.

The Meaning of 'Church'

It is better to start with the question, "What do you mean by church?" And here, in the face of widely varying interpretations among Christians, there is relative clarity in the Bible.

The word 'church' translates the Greek *ekklesia* (from which we get words like 'ecclesiastical'). In the New Testament, however, an *ekklesia* is not a religious institution but simply a gathering or assembly. In Acts 19, for example, we find that it refers both to the riot in Ephesus (19:32,41) and to the Town Council (19:39). But *ekklesia* does have a theological pedigree, having been used in the Septuagint (the earliest Greek version of the Old Testament) to translate the Hebrew *qahal*. This word also meant an assembly, but the assembly which took priority over all others in the Old Testament was that at Mt Sinai (beginning in Exodus 19) where God gave the Law to his people through Moses. In Deut 9:10, Moses calls this event "the day of the assembly".

Other gatherings, such as armies, could also be referred to as an 'assembly', but when applied to the nation, *qahal* frequently carried this sense of Israel as an assembly gathered to do business before God. It was therefore significant that Jesus picked *ekklesia* (the Greek equivalent) to describe the community that he would establish (e.g. Matt 16:18, 18:17).

This suggests that for the Christian every meeting is the assembly of God's people gathered to do business before him. But more than this, Heb 12:18-24 shows that a straight line could be drawn between the ordinary assembly of Christians and the special day of the assembly at Sinai. Our meetings are therefore great occasions – on a par with that awesome meeting at the mountain

What is the Church For?

The Bible does, of course, apply certain images to the people of God, describing them, for example, as the body and bride of Christ (1 Cor 12:27; 2 Cor 11:2). Nevertheless, these are primarily metaphors describing the church. The church 'in itself' is the assembly of God's people, so that 'church' is not so much an institution as an event. When God's people assemble they 'church' together. When we are dispersed we are still 'of the church', although we are not 'in the church'.

As Jesus observed , the 'quorum' for such an assembly or church is only two – provided a certain purpose is involved in relation to himself: "For where two or three are gathered in my name, there am I in the midst of them" (Matt 18:20). The purpose of the church, however, is not to do things which benefit God. Paul's observation in Acts 17:24-25 should control our thinking in this respect:

> *The God who made the world and everything in it, being Lord of heaven and earth, does not live in shrines made by man, nor is he served by human hands, as though he needed anything, since he himself gives to all men life and breath and everything.*

Instead, as with the assembly at Mt Sinai, the purpose of church is to benefit the people of God through hearing His word (Deut 4:1 cf. Heb 12:24) and expressing the covenant life of his people. In the church, therefore, it is not only the 'vertical relationship with God which is important. Indeed, we can express and experience this personal relationship with God in isolation.

The church also creates 'horizontal' relationships between believers (see also Eph 2:13-16) which are expressed through active love, particularly as we encourage one another in Christian living and faithfulness to the Gospel so that we may stand at last on the Day of Judgement. Hence Heb 10:24-25 urges:

...let us consider how to stir up one another to love and good works, not neglecting to meet together, as is the habit of some, but encouraging one another, and all the more as you see the Day drawing near.

Where is the Church?

If we understand this properly, we will see that the church is not just the place where Christians express their relationships with one another—it *is* those relationships. It is not just a bringing together of Christians but a relating together. Yet the church is not limited to the local gathering, for just as the Christians in a local church are members of one body, so the multitude of local churches are still the one body of Christ. You don't have more 'church' where you have more churches! We see this properly expressed in the interchangeability of ministers and members, where you can join another church without having to apply for 'membership' and be served by another minister without a new 'ordination'.

In fact, the Bible teaches that the church exists simultaneously in universal heavenly perfection and in local earthly imperfection. Thus the believer is always in the church seated with Christ in the heavenly places (Eph 2:6, cf Col 3:3) and sometimes present in an earthly church.

The duration and quality of these earthly churches vary. They can be big or small. They can exist for an hour in one place or a day in another. They can demonstrate the love of Christ and faithfulness to the Gospel or division and heresy. What makes them 'churches', however, is not their relationship to other churches, much less their relationship to certain authority figures. They are churches because of the internal relationships between individuals as members of Christ. Their relationship with other churches flows from having this in common.

Denying the Church

The earthly church therefore finds concrete expression when and where (as the Prayer Book says) "we assemble and meet together" to express the life and love of God's people—which means that churches may occur in an almost infinite variety of places and formats. The 'prayer triplet', home-group, Communion service and weekend house-party are all examples of 'church'.

Unfortunately, people often invoke unbiblical criteria in the definition of 'churches' so that they can deny the status of 'church' to a particular group. Examples include the insistence that they should include a variety of ages, that they should reflect the social pattern of the neighbourhood (itself an arbitrary concept), or that they should have elders (cf Acts 14:23, where existing churches are without elders). The classic example in the Church of England is the legal stipulation that Holy Communion can only take place when an episcopally ordained presbyter is there to say certain words. The only consolation is that when Holy Communion is celebrated in this fashion it is scarcely the great occasion for building horizontal relationships created by the fellowship meals (the *agapé*) that the first Christians had together. Congregations who wish to enjoy this fellowship may, of course, still do so, accompanying it with appropriate readings and prayers and so by their unity and purpose proclaiming the Lord's death.

This kind of thinking is now popular, or implied, of congregations that are without a minister. The implication is that in an interregnum, the congregation is not a 'proper' church. This suggestion disempowers local congregations and treats ordinary Christians like children when they happen not to be served by an official presbyter at a given moment. It is clearly ridiculous that a priest in an empty building is called a church, and five hundred people in a building without a priest is called an interregnum.

Who's in control?

Of course, the point of all this is the control of power. If you have to possess a certain qualification to be a church, the people giving out the qualifications hold the power. And if those qualifications are unbiblical then the church is controlled unbiblically. Unfortunately, this is frequently what happens within the Church of England, so that individual Christians and churches have constantly to face the tension between the demands of the denomination and the application of biblical principles.

Living in the Denomination

To deal with this tension we have to understand first that a denomination is not a church (much less is it *the* church!). On the one hand, the denomination never gathers as an actual assembly, and is therefore not a *particular* church. On the other hand, the denomination excludes other denominations, and is thus not the universal church.

However, it is perhaps not quite right either to say that the denomination is 'a federation of churches', since this puts too much stress on the separation of congregations, leaving us open to the charge of congregationalism. Instead, the denomination consists of particular individuals who 'church' with others under the denominational umbrella. But even if we avoid congregationalism, denominationalism can easily become a greater problem. Toward others, the denomination can act as if it were the only church. Towards its own members, the denomination can treat its constituent churches as if they only existed by its permission.

We see these problems in current Anglican thinking about bishops. Increasingly we are told that the definition of church is "the diocese gathered around its chief pastor and sacramental minister, the diocesan bishop" (*Church Times* 5 July 1996). Yet such a definition of church is clearly false. On the one hand, it blithely ignores all those denominations and churches which don't have bishops, or which have different bishops. On the other hand, the gathering it speaks of is entirely hypothetical – it never actually takes place! The basis for this definition is, of course, the desire to empower the bishop to control every local Anglican church which is actually gathered around Christ.

Living with the Denomination

Given this situation, many people are tempted to give up and leave the denomination. A key reason for not doing so, however, must surely be to preserve what is left of the visible unity of the Body of Christ. Admittedly denominations institutionalise both unity and disunity. They prevent us falling further apart, and they prevent us coming back together. But the solution is not to add to the problem unnecessarily.

What is needed is a boldness to live within the denomination, affirming its unity while denying its denominationalism. And this is possible because all the things which distinguish one denomination from another are either essential for the *whole* church of God or unnecessary for *any* church of God.

Let me explain. The Roman Catholic Church is entirely logical in this respect. It insists that it, and only it, is the true church and all denominations are less than churches. As Anglicans we must either take the same view, insisting that where others (such as Roman Catholics) differ from us they are wrong, or we must accept that our differences are indifferent – in which case they are indifferent inside the denomination as well as outside.

Therefore, if ordination by a bishop is necessary for a valid celebration of Holy Communion it is either necessary for all—in which case Anglicans would insist no Baptist ever actually partook of the Lord's Supper – or it is indifferent and can be ignored by those within Anglicanism who can ignore it with a good conscience. For these people, expressing the life of the Body of Christ will be more important than observing Canon B12. Moreover, they will not be unduly troubled since the denomination itself clearly does not believe that episcopal ordination is essential according to the Word of God. But they will not leave the denomination over this since they don't wish to fragment the Body of Christ any further.

Power to the Laity!

If Anglicans in general, and evangelical Anglicans in particular, began to live as free Christians within a denominational framework, what would happen when we started to break the rules? In the good old days, the consequences could be truly dreadful, including imprisonment, torture and death. We must not forget that, in this respect, we live in very easy times.

The obvious consequence is that various forms of 'discipline' would be invoked, beginning with a dressing-down by the bishop. This is hardly a fearful prospect in most cases. More seriously, ministers who encourage such dissent could be placed on the 'Lambeth List' – a blacklist of clergy – which might damage their future job prospects. On the other hand, in some circles it might enhance it. There is also the increasing likelihood that rebellious parishes will be denied a new minister when the old one dies or moves on. It is at this point – and in the provision of ministry generally – that serious action will become necessary. It is also here that the nerve of the laity needs to be strongest.

Lay people need to remember, and the Anglican hierarchy needs to learn, that Anglicanism is *a voluntary association*. It is also an association which accords considerable (albeit limited) powers to lay representatives such as church wardens. Furthermore, it is today an association whose day-to-day funding depends on lay giving. A study of the past shows that lay people have the power to alter church history. What is awaited in the present are lay people with the nerve to do it again.

The church thrives on patronage. Not the patronage of sleepy committee members who wake up once a decade to appoint an incumbent, but patrons like Frederick the Wise who provided an armed guard for Martin Luther, or the Countess of Huntingdon who opened evangelical chapels and a theological college at her own expense. And patrons need not be just the rich and powerful. For if the local church of ordinary people have clear, biblical convictions about their status and power within the denomination, and are prepared to stand against the system, the denomination may yet be preserved for the Gospel. Without such people, dissenting clergy are an easy target. With them, great things are possible, because the church is as much yours as anyone's.

WHOSE CHURCH IS IT ANYWAY?

When preparing to employ a new minister, PCCs often draw up a wish list of personal characteristics. What kind of CV does the Bible suggest that our ministers have?

CHAPTER 2

What kind of minister does our church need?

The founders of the Anglican Church—the 16th century Reformers—understood the ordained minister to be a preacher of the Gospel and a teacher of the Word. This is strongly reflected in the Ordinal at the end of the Book of Common Prayer and in the Book of Homilies. It was emphasised by giving to the new deacon or presbyter not a chalice or paten for Holy Communion, but a Bible, with which to teach the God's Word.

In the 17th century, the Puritans added two further priorities. The minister was also to be a physician of the soul and a pastor of the flock. This pattern was exemplified by someone such as Richard Baxter of Kidderminster, and the Puritans had great systems of biblical counselling. With the Evangelical Revival in the 18th century, the minister also became an organiser of outreach and a mediator of fellowship. This is seen very clearly in the Methodist classes that John and Charles Wesley started in order to provide fellowship, prayer and Bible study.

In the 19th century, there were giants in the land—J C Ryle on the Anglican side and C H Spurgeon from the Free Churches. They did all these things their predecessors had done and this was possibly the noblest and loftiest tradition of the ordained ministry that the world has seen. Sadly it is an impossible, unrealistic model and has the major defect of raising expectations for an omnicompetent minister who becomes a bottleneck, with the laity inevitably lapsing into passivity.

What we need to do is to rediscover the biblical pattern, and the rest of this paper will point to some guidelines. We do not, if truth be told, like a distinction between clergy and laity, and at the same time we recognise the full and vital ministry of all members of Christ's Church—lay and clerical, male and female—but in what follows we shall be thinking of the one who is set apart to lead the local congregation, usually an incumbent, vicar or rector.

It is well known that in the New Testament the leaders and officials of the Christian Church are called elders, overseers, fishermen, shepherds, deacons and servants, but never once priests. The priestly function of the tribe of Levi in the Old Testament was not transferred to the New Testament's ministers. The priesthood is fulfilled in and by Christ, and, in a secondary sense, by all God's people. The Christian Church does not have a priesthood, it *is* a priesthood. Because the desire—and expectation—of the natural man is to have such a priestly class, we shall always need to make a stand against it.

The New Testament gives us three books (the Pastoral Epistles) in which the role and function of the Christian minister are explained. There is a deafening silence on certain issues which we might have expected to be included. For instance, there is nothing said about taking services or visiting the sick or celebrating Holy Communion or chairing committees. Rather there is first and foremost a great emphasis on moral characteristics so that the minister is to model the Christian qualities of love, hospitality, patience, self-control (especially in the areas of alcohol, money, sex and temper).

The one non-moral quality that is required, however, is that the minister is to be a faithful man and able to teach. This has two sides to it. In the first place he is meant to be faithful to sound doctrine—that is to the 'deposit'—"the faith once for all delivered to the saints." The Pastoral Letters have this great emphasis on guarding and keeping the Gospel— which cannot be altered, subtracted from, added to or developed. The theological understanding and position of the minister is therefore of vital importance. This is why the Reformers insisted that ministers—but not all members of the congregation—subscribed to the Thirty-nine Articles.

However, it is not enough to be faithful for the minister must also be able to teach. What sometimes happens is that one finds Christian leaders who are very able—possibly great—communicators but they are no longer faithful. At the same time there will be ministers who are very faithful and worthy, but who do not have great teaching ability. Therefore, aptitude in teaching is fundamental. This is how pastoring is done. The New Testament would not understand us if we said of somebody, 'he's not a good teacher, but he's very good pastorally' or vice versa, 'he's hopeless pastorally, but he's a great preacher.'

The strong emphasis on the ministry of the Word being the key task for the leader of the local church may surprise some, but it is consequent of a very high view of the Word of God and what this ministry of the Word produces.

This is well spelt out in Ephesians 4. We read that the ascended Christ gave four 'word gifts' to the Church—namely apostles and prophets (foundational gifts in Ephesians), evangelists and pastor/teachers. When the pastor/teacher (one and the same person) does his job properly, the following results should be evident:

1. EVERY MEMBER MINISTRY: Ephesians 4:12

When the minister recovers his proper ministry—namely teaching the Bible—he recovers for the laity their ministry and the minister is no longer the omnicompetent bottleneck. The minister doesn't necessarily need to go on management courses or work a lap-top computer, but if he is gifted and faithful in teaching the Bible then the saints are equipped and begin their work and ministry, without which they will always be frustrated and the work of the Gospel will falter.

2. UNITY: Ephesians 4:13

This is one of the big themes of the chapter. We all know that one of the Devil's favourite tricks is to get a congregation divided or split into factions. The lie then goes round, "Christ unites; doctrine divides....don't be too tight on doctrine; it causes splits in fellowship". The New Testament takes exactly the opposite line, and says that unity is to be found in the truth, as we are to be 'of one mind'. In Ephesians 4:4-7 we see our unity is trinitarian. We have the Spirit, the Lord Jesus and the Father. We must be united in a future expectation of the Kingdom of God—v4, "one body and one Spirit just as we were called in one hope"—that is, united in a belief and a confidence that if we're Christian people we're heading for heaven. United, too, in the uniqueness and supremacy of the Lord Jesus—v5, one Lord—that is, our understanding of the total deity of the Lord Jesus Christ—and his exclusivity. United, furthermore, in confidence that salvation is only by grace—that's what lies behind the phrase 'one faith' (v5). We can do nothing to earn it. We must trust in what the Lord Jesus has done for us. We are united in the personal experience of new birth and must make public testimony of it—that is what is meant by 'one baptism' (v5). We are united in our adoption as sons—"there is one God and Father of us all". This passage is full of doctrinal content. These truths are non-negotiable. It is on this central teaching that unity is built and it is the pastor/teacher who teaches these truths and so promotes unity.

There are, of course, secondary issues, and there can be a danger of majoring on minors—such as the amount of water used in baptism, the form of church government, a particular line for or against the charismatic gifts, a particular view of the millennium. The 'proportion' of Scripture is an important principle here, ie, the weight that Scripture places on a certain doctrine, by the amount of space it gives to it. This should be reflected in the pattern and emphasis of our own teaching.

3. MATURITY: Ephesians 4:13

It is tragic when a child doesn't grow up and is stunted physically, emotionally, or mentally. Sadly some Christians and congregations do not go on to spiritual maturity. The mark of the immature person is that they are too easily rocked and knocked off balance by new winds of doctrine— usually blowing across the Atlantic and being hastily produced in paperback. The safeguard against all the conflicting views that are circling round today—even under the name of evangelicalism—is a thorough grounding in the Scriptures. Once again the pastor/teacher is the key for that grounding, and therefore to spiritual maturity.

4. EVANGELISM: Ephesians 4:17-20

Ephesians expresses conversion in a striking way. The mark of a pagan is that his thinking is all wrong. The Christian believer is someone who has '"learnt Christ". To learn Christ I need a teacher. Although on some rare occasions the New Testament envisages the office of an evangelist, generally the pastor/teacher must be his own evangelist, for by teaching the Bible he is engaging in evangelism. It is fair to say that just about every church meeting should be seen as a Gospel opportunity, and the teaching of the Bible by the pastor/teacher must go hand-in-hand with the personal evangelism that he and the other members of the congregation engage in.

5. HOLINESS: Ephesians 5:22

Christ-like living is not produced by constant exhortation but by a steady teaching of the truth. Holy living is—in the Bible—the response to theological truths. This is clear from the Ten Commandments and from Mark 12:29. It is also a great theme of the Pastorals—c.f. Titus 1:1— "knowledge of the truth which accords with godliness". One of the reasons that so much emphasis is laid on the moral characteristics of the minister in the Pastorals is that if his lifestyle is defective, it must mean that his doctrine is defective, because the two go hand-in-hand. If therefore we want a congregation that reflects the beauty of the Lord Jesus, so that we're known as gracious, considerate, loving neighbours—what we need is a pastor who will teach the truth!

So what a congregation should look for in a new minister is not primarily a social worker and certainly not a priest. He must of course, be a friend, caring and given to hospitality. Supremely, though, he must be a teacher. Once he has been appointed, he must be set free to make teaching the Bible his priority. He must not be telephoned during study hours; he should be given a book grant; he must be encouraged to go on 'in-service' training in expository preaching. He must be verbally encouraged—that is, thanked when he expounds faithfully. For the preacher to see people under the pulpit taking notes is a great incentive to more careful preparation. Let him stick to his task and don't let him dissipate his energies in secondary matters. The congregation will then be set free for their ministry.

If your church is about to be, or is, in an interregnum, then use biblical criteria as the basis of your choice of the new minister, and do not accept his word that he is "an evangelical". At a time when a wide spectrum of clergy are talking about commitment to Christ, evangelism, mission and the like, it is possible to end up appointing a wolf in sheep's clothing. Similarly, resist pressures to take this man, or that, because external sources are intent on finding him a job! By all means meet him, hear him out on the way he sees his ministry but if he does not operate from the New Testament principles spelled out above, say a polite 'no thank-you' and continue prayerfully to seek out a man who does.

How can you be sure that you are appointing the right person? Sadly, many churches have found to their dismay that the minister who seemed to have all the right credentials and to give the right answers at the interview turns out to be very different when he is firmly settled in the vicarage. No interview method is foolproof, but this chapter is designed to help you ask the kind of probing questions which will reveal any hidden agendas

CHAPTER 3

Searching questions

It is with considerable hesitation that we make suggestions for possible lines of questioning. Interviews should always be good natured and caring, and although some of the following ideas for questions may seem a little stark on the printed page, we want to stress that they should be asked with gentleness, graciousness, humility, sensitivity and humour. Some subtlety may also be required, as the interviewee may have been briefed by someone who has seen these questions!

I would like to suggest that you need to discover in detail what makes the candidate tick in five different areas:

1. THEOLOGY
• *What is your Gospel?*
It may seem wildly obvious, but it is remarkable how often this vital area is explored in relatively little depth in an interview compared with the more practical details such as housing. You should look out to make sure that their Gospel is God-centred rather than man-centred, and that its heart is the substitutionary death of the Lord Jesus satisfying the holy righteousness of God.

• *How do you regard the Bible?*
We would look for answers that show that they regard the Bible as supreme over, for example, tradition and reason, and also sufficient for all matters of faith and conduct *and* for its own interpretation.

• *What do you feel about the ordination of women?*
If for: • *Do you respect the two integrities?**
        • *How long do you think the two integrities
         model will be needed*
If against: • *How will you encourage ministry by women among women?*

---

* The Church of England explicitly states that the minority view that women should not be ordained should be respected. This is known as the 'two integrities'.

• *What are your views on the work of the Holy Spirit?*
You will need to be especially cautious here, as it is possible to use the
right language to mean many different things. No-one will say that they are
'closed to the Holy Spirit', but a little digging may be needed to work out
exactly what they mean by the statements they give, for example:

• *How will you avoid giving the impression that conversion is two-stage
and that there are first and second-class Christians?*

• *How will you deal sensitively and positively with those within the
congregation who have different opinions from you on the subject?*

• *How central do you regard the doctrine of the Trinity?* and
• *How would you teach it to children?*
Watch out for the heresies of Unitarianism and Sabellianism!
(Unitarianism teaches that the Father is God, and that Jesus and the Spirit
are less so. Sabellianism defines the different members of the Trinity by
their roles, rather than their persons.)

• *What is your teaching on homosexuality?*
Look out for firmness, humility and compassion.

You may also want to ask further questions about 'churchmanship', e.g.
views on baptism, robes/vestments, and the Holy Communion, which are
more specific to your usual way of doing things.

• *What is the hardest pastoral problem you have had to deal with? Why
was it so hard for you? How did you deal with it?*

2. PASTORAL
• *What are your priorities in ministry?*
We would hope that these would include the following:

I. Expository Preaching.
• *How long does it take you to prepare a sermon?*
a rule of thumb might be that a 30 minute sermon should involve
10 hours prep

• *Tell us some of the books you have read recently*
you would hope to hear that he has read some serious Bible commentaries.

• *Would you value a 'reading week' each year?*
a positive response here would be good as there is never enough time to
study.

• *What in-service training and conferences have you been on recently?*
if he goes on counselling courses rather than on preaching courses, you'll
discover where his priorities really lie.)

II. Evangelism.

• *Tell us about your own personal and public evangelistic ministry*
you will be attracted to a minister who both preaches and practises
evangelism.

• *How do you keep in touch with non-Christian friends?*
Ensure that his personal work isn't just crisis/problem oriented, and that he
can teach the Bible one-to-one over a period of time.

3. LEADERSHIP

• *We definitely want a leader, but there are many different styles of
leadership. What sort of autocrat are you?*

• *Describe how you would go about making decisions and policy for the
church.*

• *How will you initiate and manage change?*

• *What level of involvement would you want to have with church
committees? Do you want to be on every one? Will you want to chair the
Church Council? Will you want to lead all the services? Will you want to
preach all the sermons?*

Most clergy *say* that they believe in 'every member ministry', but very few
in practice surrender their powers on matters of finance or policy making.
It would be good to establish how power sharing is going to take place
from the very beginning. It never seems important until a crisis arrives, but
then it is often too late to remedy the situation.

4. THE WIDER CHURCH

• *How do you see the Church of England at the moment?*

• *What do you hope your involvement will be in the Deanery/Diocese/ General Synod? Would you expect to serve on other groups such as the Evangelical Alliance, Eclectics, or on committees of mission agencies?*

• *Do you intend to accept many 'away fixtures' – speaking engagements on conferences, weekends or at other churches? How do you decide which ones to accept?*

Good to get an indication on these areas as your minister may be more absent than present...

• *Tell us about your interest in overseas mission.*

• *Which mission agencies/countries do you have a special interest in?*

5. PERSONAL

In order to be faithful to instructions in the Pastoral Epistles, in addition to verifying that the candidate teaches the truth, we need to sensitively probe their personal life. Often the doctrinal position of the candidate is determined by listening to sermon tapes or by visiting the current church. Personal matters, however, need to be handled **very discreetly.** Possibly, one member of the panel could ask the necessary questions privately. However it is handled, you need to be sure that the areas of money, sex, alcohol and temper are under control, and that there are, as far as you can ascertain, no unresolved personal problems from the past. Ask, for example, about their childhood and adolescence.

• *What do you do for fun?*

• *What interests do you have outside the work of the Gospel and the congregation?*

• *What pattern have you developed for your devotional life?*

• *Tell us about your family.*
If single, then an understanding of any family network and support is
important. The single candidate needs to be asked what support group he
already has and what he expects. It may also be judicious to ask if he is
looking to marry, and how he would handle a relationship with a member
of the congregation, if one developed.

If married, his spouse and children should be in total sympathy with his
ministry and aims. No expectations should be made by the church as to
how involved the wife wants to be, but their home needs to be open and
given to hospitality. A totally supportive wife is crucial, and ideally she
should be at the interview.

• *When did you last take your wife out for a treat?*

• *Do you have a day off, and what do you do with it?*

• *How do you teach your faith to your children?*

• *What are your hopes for your children?*
you discover their *real* ambitions by what they want for their kids

For most of us, the intricacies of the legal system are best left to those who know, because a little knowledge is often a dangerous thing. No knowledge, however, can be even more disastrous. Understanding the nature of legal responsibilities for your church buildings and the nature of your minister's terms of appointment are vital, however, if you are to fight your corner over appointments.

CHAPTER 4

Filling the Gap: the legal position

1. INTRODUCTION

There is considerable ignorance among lay people of the mysterious process by which appointments of clergymen are made within the Church of England. There are a number of reasons for this. The infrequency of such appointments discourages laymen and in particular PCCs from becoming "boned up" on what they perceive as an esoteric subject with which they may never have to deal. Furthermore, the legislation which governs the appointment process seems inaccessible, complicated, and full of unfamiliar terminology. In practice, therefore, if they ever do have to get involved in the appointment process, there is a temptation for lay people to leave these matters to the professionals—the patron and the bishop—and themselves to play a purely passive role in the appointment process.

Reform believes that this is a pity and results from a fundamental misunderstanding of the importance which the legislation attaches to the role of lay people—in particular the elected representatives of the PCC—in the appointment of a new vicar or rector. The purpose of this chapter is to try shed some light on the subject. It cannot possibly be exhaustive in dealing with all the different variants and complexities that might arise but if it points people in the direction of where they can obtain further help— either from source materials or from people with experience in these areas—then it will have served its purpose.

Although there are more detailed works on this subject, some of which are mentioned in the Sources section, this paper unashamedly looks at the appointments question from the point of view of the lay person, whether church warden, member of the PCC, or the PCC's elected representatives. In any one of these capacities you may have an important role to play in the appointment of your new vicar or rector. The more you know about your responsibilities, rights and duties, the better able you will be to fulfil them when the time comes.

2. MAIN SOURCES
Text Books

1. *Ecclesiastical Law* by Mark Hill 1995. Published by Butterworths. £98
The authoritative and up to date legal textbook.

2. *Moores Introduction to English Canon Law* by Briden & Hanson
   Published by Mowbray. £6.99
*Contains an easy to read chapter on The Parish which includes a
description of the role of Church Wardens and of the system of
appointment of new Incumbents.*

3. *A Handbook for Church Wardens and PCCs* by MacMorran &
   Binder
A useful little paperback just republished by Mowbrays in a 1996 edition.

4. *An ABC for the PCC* by John Pitchford published by Mowbrays
   2nd revised edition 1985.

5. *Situation Vacant—A Guide to the Appointment Process in the
   Church of England* by David Parrott and David Field in the Grove
   Pastoral Series. £1.95

Legislation
   • Pastoral Measure 1983
   • Patronage (Benefices) Measure 1986
   • Canons C14 and C15 (set out in Appendix I)

3. DEFINITIONS
These are some of the words and phrases you will come into contact with.
Some will be familiar—others less so. All have a precise meaning in the
legislation.

1. **Beneficed clergy**—those holding the freehold office ie.
   incumbents, rectors, vicars.

2. **Freehold**—technically beneficed clergy are the legal owners of the
   parish church and its churchyard. Of more practical importance is
   the fact that such clergy cannot in the usual course be removed
   from office, ie. they have security of tenure.

3. **Unbeneficed clergy**—those who have no freehold office ie. priests

in charge, vicars in team ministries, assistant curates, chaplains, ministers of proprietary chapels.

4. **Cure of Souls**—within the parish is to be exercised by the incumbent, in conjunction with the diocesan bishop. Other clergy may only minister there with the incumbent's permission (Canon C8)

5. **Incumbent**—the clergyman having the exclusive cure of souls in a parish—referred to as either the rector or the vicar.

6. **Assistant Curates**—unbeneficed clergy licensed by the bishop on the nomination of the incumbent.

7. **Patronage**—the right to appoint a person to a benefice. May be transferred (subject to restrictions) but not sold.

8. **Register of Patrons**—of every benefice must be compiled and maintained in each Diocesan Registry. All transfers must be recorded.

9. **Parish representatives**—two people, usually but not necessarily the wardens, who are elected by the PCC to act as its representatives in the selection process of a new incumbent.

10. **Designated Officer**—nominated by the bishop: he is often either the Registrar of the Diocese or the secretary of the Pastoral Committee of the diocese.

11. **Presentation**—the patron "presents" his nominee to the bishop, so that he may be given the cure of souls in the parish.

12. **Institution into the spiritualities** (the spiritual responsibilities)— the formal commissioning of the new incumbent—usually carried out by the bishop in the parish church.

13. **Induction into the temporalities** (the bricks and mortar)—usually done by the archdeacon at the same time and place.

14. **Suspension**—by the bishop of the patron's right of presentation pursuant to the Pastoral Measure 1983.

15. **Pastoral Committee**—set up under the Pastoral Measure 1983 in order to review the arrangements for pastoral supervision in the diocese. This includes creation, alteration or dissolution of benefices and parishes in accordance with pastoral schemes.

16. **Canons**—the type of legislation which may be directly amended by general synod.

17. **Measures**—the ecclesiastical equivalent of Acts of Parliament, having the same authority. Measures are passed by General Synod and may relate to any matter concerning the Church of England.

4. PROCEDURE FOR APPOINTING A NEW INCUMBENT

Background

For administrative purposes the Church of England is divided into parishes which are geographical areas committed to an incumbent for the cure of souls. The cure of souls within the parish is to be exercised by the incumbent, in conjunction with the diocesan bishop, though the incumbent may permit other clergy to function within his benefice. Such clergy are only required to be 'of good standing' (Canon C28a). The parochial system grew out of the practice of bishops sending parsons from the cathedral to designated areas in order to preach and administer the sacraments. With the passing of time, churches were built and endowed and priests were ordained to serve in them. These historic parishes have been altered and modified to take account of social and population changes over the centuries. Nowadays, parish boundaries are of greater significance in rural areas than in the major urban centres of population.

The procedure for the appointment of a new vicar or rector is governed by the Patronage (Benefices) Measure 1986. This envisages the involvement and co-operation of three different interest groups—each with a different role to play. First of all there is the patron who has the duty of nominating or putting forward a candidate and subsequently presenting him for institution. Secondly there is the PCC, which operates through a little committee of two elected representatives, who affirm or veto the patron's nomination. Thirdly there is the bishop, also with a limited right of veto, who will eventually institute the successful candidate.

The idea is one of checks and balances rather akin to those which are worked out in the constitution between the legislature, the executive and the judiciary. Thus the patron cannot appoint a new vicar without the consent of the PCC—nor can the bishop initiate the process by nominating a candidate. Having said this, the diocesan bishop is also the patron of many churches and this necessarily affects the balance of responsibility and power because he will then exercise two out of the three roles. In such cases it is even more important for the PCC to be aware of its rights and responsibilities, to be vigilant, and to play an effective part in the appointment process.

Patrons

Historically, the right to appoint a person to a vacant benefice has become vested in patrons of whom there are three main kinds:-

(a) The Individual

These are sometimes known as "amateur" patrons. The patronage may have been passed down by will from generation to generation. They will therefore vary in commitment and outlook.

(b) The Patronage Trust or Society

Fortunately many of our predecessors donated their patronage to trusts which are usually professional and well organised. Sometimes these trusts exist to nominate incumbents for the one parish only; in other cases, they have a selection of livings in their gift. Some of the major trusts and a summary of the way in which they operate can be found at Appendix II.

(c) The bishops

In many dioceses, the bishop may have a considerable amount of patronage in his gift, e.g. in Southwark, the bishop controls approximately 50% of the churches in the diocese.

A register of patrons must be maintained in each diocese. This register is open to public inspection and registration is necessary before a patron can exercise any of his official functions. Patronages cannot be sold, although they can be transferred subject to certain procedures and safeguards (see S.3 Patronages (Benefices) Measure 1986).

The Selection Process (for beneficed clergy)

It may be helpful to set out the procedure by way of the following timetable which will start once it is known there is a vacancy, or an impending vacancy. In what follows it has been assumed that the patron is someone other than the bishop; the procedure is essentially the same, albeit somewhat streamlined, when the two functions are combined. You must be aware that there is a time factor involved. From the date your minister finishes his official duties, there is a nine-month period during which the patron must present a candidate. If after nine months either no candidate has been presented or accepted, the right of presentation passes to the archbishop of the province.

(1) The wardens should advise the bishop of the vacancy and he must give formal notice to the "designated officer" of the diocese who is required to inform the patron as well as the secretary of the PCC.

(2) The patron must make the required declaration of his status (ie. that he is a communicant member of the Church of England) within two months of being notified of the vacancy.

(3) Within four weeks of the secretary of the PCC being notified of the vacancy, it shall meet:-

(a) to prepare a "parish profile" ie. a statement describing the conditions, needs and tradition of the parish (which must be sent to the bishop and patron) and

(b) to appoint two lay members of the PCC (usually but not necessarily the wardens) to act as its representatives in the selection process. These will be referred to as "the parish representatives"

(c) to decide whether to request the patron to consider advertising the vacancy

(d) to decide whether to request a statement in writing from the bishop describing, in relation to the benefice, the needs of the diocese and the wider needs of the church

(e) to decide whether to request a meeting with the bishop at which the parish profile and the bishop's statement may be discussed with the patron. Such a meeting must be held within six weeks of the date it is requested

(f) to consider passing Resolutions A and/or B under the Priests (Ordination of Women) Measure 1993 (see Appendix III).

(4) The patron is not allowed to offer to present to the vacant benefice until the making of such offer has been approved by the parish representatives and the bishop. In other words both have a power of veto over the candidates put forward by the patron, although the grounds upon which the bishop's veto can be exercised are strictly limited (see below). The veto of the parish representatives must be on substantial grounds such as the candidate's failure to meet a significant requirement mentioned in the parish profile. If this veto is exercised, the patron must be advised in writing within 14 days stating the grounds on which their refusal is made.

(5) If approval of an offer is refused (by bishop or parish representatives) the patron may request the archbishop to review the matter on appeal. When this happens time stops running for the purposes of the appointment (the nine month gestation period).

(6) Where an offer is made to a candidate, the patron is required to send a notice to the bishop presenting the priest for admission to the benefice.

Bishop's Refusal

The bishop may refuse to institute a presentee but his right to do so is strictly limited. It may only be exercised in the following circumstances:

(a) if there was a change of patron during the year preceding the vacancy

(b) if not more than three years have passed since the presentee was made deacon

(c) if the presentee is unfit through illness "serious and pecuniary embarrassment" or "scandal concerning his moral character"

(d) if the presentee has had less than three years experience as a full time parochial minister.

There is a right of appeal against a refusal by the bishop to institute which may be exercised either by the patron or the presentee. The appellate tribunal comprises the archbishop of the province and the Dean of the Arches or Auditor. There is no appeal from this tribunal.

Default
If the patron, parish representatives and the bishop fail to agree on the new candidate and no presentation is made within nine months of the vacancy, the right of presentation passes to the archbishop of the province.

Presentation, Institution and Induction
Once the candidate has been chosen, the patron "presents" his nominee to the bishop so that he may be given the cure of souls in the parish. The bishop must then serve three weeks notice on the church wardens stating his intention to "institute" the new clergyman and church wardens are required to publish this notice. After that period, the institution should take place as soon as possible, ideally in the parish church. Before admission the presentee must take the oaths of obedience to the Queen and of canonical obedience to the bishop which are prescribed in Canons 13 and 14 as well as making the Declaration of Assent set out in Canon 15.

Suspension of the Right of Presentation
Section 67 of the Pastoral Measure 1983 enables a bishop to suspend the right of presentation for a period of up to five years and this is renewable for further periods of up to five years. The power can only be exercised where a benefice is, or shortly to become, vacant. The consent of the Pastoral Committee has to be obtained and the bishop must consult with:
(a) the patron
(b) the PCC
(c) the chairman of the deanery synod.

The important thing to remember is that the bishop must inform those whom he is obliged to consult of the reasons why he is considering exercising his power of suspension. Furthermore, the people with whom the bishop must consult can demand a meeting with him. Such a meeting may be a better means of communicating your views as well as finding out everything on the bishop's agenda and the reasons he is considering suspension.

Although the Pastoral Measure itself is silent about the reasons why the bishop may suspend a right of presentation, guidance about this is given in "The Pastoral Measure Code of Recommended Practice" which states as follows:

"It is further recommended that use of these powers should, in the main, be confined to benefices where pastoral reorganisation is under consideration or in progress, and that use should be for limited periods only."

Theoretically, once the right of presentation has been suspended, the bishop has the power to appoint the new clergyman who will be the priest in charge as opposed to the incumbent. In other words he will not have the freehold, will not therefore have any security of tenure, possessing only a fixed-term contract, under which he is answerable to the bishop. The above provisions for the selection of beneficed clergy (including the right of veto) will therefore not apply to the appointment of the priest in charge. Having said this, the PCC should remain in close consultation with the bishop over the appointment of the priest in charge and make it clear whom their desired candidate is. In this way they may yet exert considerable influence over that appointment.

It needs to be noted that where the patron is not the bishop, if the diocese wishes to impose a priest-in-charge (which is possible) the patron does not have to sanction this appointment or present the priest-in-charge to the benefice when the suspension is lifted. As suspensions cannot continue indefinitely there comes a time when the diocese has to ask the patron to confirm the appointment and if this appointment has been imposed the patron has the absolute right to say "No". It is therefore wiser for the diocese to work with the patron and the parish otherwise the diocese could be severely embarrassed.

The Role of Women

Following the passage of the Priests (Ordination of Women) Measure 1993, parishes are allowed to pass either one or both of two Resolutions declining to accept a woman as the presiding minister or as the incumbent, as the case may be. Any parish which considers that a vacancy may occur in the short to medium term ought to consider voting upon Resolutions A and B at the earliest opportunity, for without them, the parish has no right to discriminate against the appointment of a woman as incumbent. The relevant part of the text of the Bishops Directions for the implementation of the Episcopal Ministry Act for the Diocese of Southwark is set out in Appendix III.

5. PRACTICAL HINTS

It is one thing to know in theory how the system works or should work. It

37

is quite another to "work the system" to best advantage. The objective is to employ the best qualified candidate and to obtain a match between his gifts, skills and talents and the needs and requirements of your particular parish. With that aim in mind, the following "twenty tips" are offered with PCCs, wardens and parish representatives very much in mind:

1. **Don't forget the timescale you are operating within.** The gestation period for the new appointment is not hard to remember— it is a mere nine months. Both the wardens and the patron have every incentive to make an appointment within that period as neither should want the archbishop of the province to take over and be given the right of presentation. However, remember that the clock only starts running when the outgoing incumbent actually retires, ie his last official working day, even though the diocese may send out preparatory papers to you before that date.

2. **Maintain good relations.** Although some of what follows assumes a less than perfect accord with one's patron and/or bishop, there is obviously no substitute for a good working personal relationship fostered by respect and politeness at all times even (especially) when the going gets tough. The more you listen the more opportunity you have of analysing the arguments and facts being presented. Don't be afraid to make jottings to remind you of points being made so that when you speak your analysis will be accurate, coherent and well argued. In such a climate differences of approach or view can often be discussed amicably and resolved without conflict.

3. **Know the law.** There are no short cuts in this area. If you do not know how the system works, you are liable to be at the mercy of others who do. Remember that the bishops have, by the very nature of their appointment, demonstrated a certain skill in these areas and can be expected to have not only the requisite knowledge but also the experience of having already handled a considerable number of new appointments. Your ability to cite accurately and in detail the relevant legislation and to understand its implications will give you powerful levers to unsettle clerical assumptions of lay compliance.

4. **Take the initiative.** In most cases PCC will have advance knowledge of an impending vacancy and can therefore be formulating thoughts and plans before any of the formal steps are

taken. There is nothing underhand about this. It is simply a case of forewarned is forearmed. You will find it helpful to use this time constructively, ideally in consultation with the patron.

5. **Do your homework.** In particular, take the following action:

   (a) Formulate a clear idea of the kind of person you are looking for.
   (b) Subject to questions of confidentiality, ask around the evangelical grapevine. Word of mouth and personal recommendation often produce excellent leads.
   (c) If you are aware of possible candidates, go and hear them preach (more than once) and try and find out "the views from the pews" in the candidate's existing church. At the outset, this may have to be done anonymously.

6. **Be well organised.** Keep copies of letters sent and retain all letters received. File all such correspondence chronologically and ensure that all concerned have the same file which should contain all other relevant documents such as trust deeds and copies of the relevant legislation.

7. **Draft a good parish profile.** Remember you are searching for an excellent candidate who may have a number of opportunities open to him. Your profile may be the first introduction a candidate has to your church and if it is well produced, this will speak volumes about the quality of the lay leadership. Having said this be frank; do not be tempted to exaggerate strengths or minimise weaknesses. The most important part of the profile is the job description which should spell out very clearly your wish to appoint an evangelical and any other requirements that are important to your church. This will be relevant to the use your veto, should you wish to use it.

8. **Advertise widely.** Most churches wait for the patron to suggest candidates. However there is nothing to stop you from suggesting candidates to him and liaising closely with him over the question of advertising. Furthermore, the parish representatives can require the patron to advertise the vacancy if they wish. As the patron may only be prepared to put forward one candidate at a time, this approach may procure a greater number of candidates from which you can make your selection.

9. **Get on with it.** Diocesan finances are such that some patrons have been discouraged by their bishops from advertising for some six months or more after the vacancy occurs. Such delay is inconsistent with the statutory timetable and is unjustifiable. Ensure you keep the momentum going.

10. **Watch out for "ring-fencing".** Your bishop may decline to consider a candidate unless he is already employed within the diocese. Again, this is a policy born of financial constraints, which finds no support in the legislation. There is no reason at all why you should not consider candidates from outside the diocese.

11. **Remember the Caution List.** The bishops have access to an unofficial list which records serious black marks against clergy. Such clergy are therefore unlikely to be acceptable to patron or bishop.

12. **Develop a shrewd interviewing policy.** The traditional method has been to see one candidate at a time and only if one rejects the first, does one see the second and so on. This method can waste a lot of time. The alternative is to shortlist, say, three candidates. There are advocates of both policies. Advantages of the first are that confidentiality is maintained, and it avoids the risk of choosing those who shine at interview, but who may not necessarily be the best candidate. On the other hand do you think it is important to be able to make a comparative assessment of all the candidates? A middle course may be to interview three candidates over three days.

13. **Sharpen up your interviewing techniques.** The decision of the parish representatives is critical for the future of your church. It is therefore essential to have a clear idea of what you want to find out from each candidate and the ability to probe politely behind the somewhat clichéd exchanges which can so easily characterise these occasions. Thus, avoid leading questions and ask in some detail about his views about preaching programmes and his method of sermon preparation. Assess the man on what he says—not on what you think you heard or wanted to hear.

14. **Give it time.** After you have heard the candidates preach and completed the interviewing formalities you may think it wise to

share a relaxed meal with the candidates and, ideally, their wives, followed by prayer together.

15. **Be realistic.** We all want to employ someone who, besides being a superb preacher, is also an outstanding evangelist, a super sensitive pastor, a brilliant administrator, a computer whiz and a diocesan diplomat, all rolled into one. He does not exist. Identify your priorities, and be prepared to settle for someone other than the Archangel Gabriel.

16. **Beware of the hidden agenda.** Many bishops have excellent records as patrons but they will necessarily have wider concerns within the diocese eg. of promoting their own brand of churchmanship. It would be wise to get to know your bishop well, particularly if he is the patron, and try and understand the various practical and political considerations that he is likely to have in mind in relation to the appointment. At the same time be aware of his own public doctrinal confession as set out in the Declaration of Assent in C.15. This is set out in Appendix I.

16. **Don't be overawed.** Remember that in this process the real power lies with the parish representatives (who have the veto) rather than the bishop (who in most cases does not). Therefore be resolute and prepared to subject to critical scrutiny all the facts and explanations given to you—keeping a wary eye out for inconsistences.

17. **Ask for reasons.** If a patron (of whatever kind) is unwilling to put forward a candidate that you have suggested, request a meeting so that the reasons can been fully explored. In the same way, if the bishop refuses to approve the making of an offer to a candidate who has been put forward by the patron and approved by the parish representatives, he must notify the patron in writing of the grounds upon which the refusal is made. Ask to see a copy of his letter. It then becomes hard for the bishop to hide behind an inadmissible reason for objecting to a candidate such as his doctrinal orthodoxy.

18. **Avoid litigating or using the media if at all possible.** However, we are talking about Gospel issues here and it may therefore be right that these tactics should be resorted to but only as remedies of last resort.

20. **Pray unceasingly** recognising that we are trying to do God's will, not our own and that He is Sovereign. Pray individually and collectively as a church for wisdom, patience and love, not just for your church but for all others involved, patron, bishop and candidates.

6. A CASE HISTORY

It can be instructive and encouraging to learn from the experience of others. Here is an example of an actual situation which occurred not so long ago; as seen from the perspective of the applicant:

"Not long ago I was looking for an incumbency in the Church of England. I came into contact with the patrons—a charitable trust—of a vacant parish that sounded a promising possibility. It was agreed that I would take an initial look and report back. After the first contact we felt that this might well be God's place for us.

At this point we hit a problem. The diocese in which the parish lay had a policy of only appointing from within the diocese. The patrons had obediently followed this instruction for about nine months. Now, having exhausted suitable candidates from within the diocese, they were looking outside.

The person acting on behalf of the trust now wrote to the bishop to inform him that I was looking at the position. He received a fax on the day his letter was received telling him that the appointment was out of the question.

We decided that we would ignore this directive and I went for interview in the parish. I was invited to come as minister and accepted. The secretary of the Trust now wrote to the bishop to say that they were going to nominate me for the living.

Soon after, while I was away on a conference, I had a message to ring the bishop. I duly telephoned and he asked me to come and see him. I wasn't sure why he wanted to see me and said "Do you mean that the appointment can go ahead?" Imagine my surprise when he said "Oh yes, we've always known that we haven't a legal leg to stand on with our policy of appointments from within the diocese". He then asked me not to let the cat out of the bag!

It was striking that it was a small trust (as this one was) which was willing to take on the diocese whereas the large trusts had meekly toed the line. When I remonstrated with the secretary of one of these large trusts about this he said: "Yes, we must start taking them on". But why were they not blazing the trail? Why was it left to a small trust to act so courageously?"

7. CONCLUSION

The purpose of this chapter is to encourage you to be proactive and to help you to be prepared in relation to the most important decision your church is likely to face—the appointment of its new minister. The underlying assumption of what has been said is that the laity have tended to abdicate their proper role in that process. Reform believes that it is of vital and strategic importance for the effective proclamation of the Gospel that parish representatives should once again exercise their responsibility in this area effectively.

Finally, please remember that everything stated here is only a general summary of the law and practice in this area. There is no substitute for particular advice about specific situations and the Reform Office at Christ Church, Fulwood, Canterbury Avenue, Sheffield S10 3RT, tel 0114 230 1911, fax 0114 230 6568 will be pleased to put you in touch with people who may be able to give further informal advice, in confidence, should you require it.

APPENDIX I
Canons relating to obedience and assent

C14 OF THE OATHS OF OBEDIENCE

1. Every person whose election to any bishopric is to be confirmed, or who is to be consecrated bishop or translated to any bishopric or suffragan bishopric, shall first take the oath of due obedience to the archbishop and to the metropolitical Church of the Province wherein he is to exercise the episcopal office in the form and manner prescribed in and by the Ordinal.
2. Either archbishop consecrating any person to exercise episcopal functions elsewhere than in England may dispense with the said oath.
3. Every person who is to be ordained priest or deacon, or to be instituted to any benefice, or to be licensed either to any lectureship, preachership, or stipendiary curacy, or to serve in any place, shall first take the Oath of Canonical obedience to the bishop of the diocese by whom he is to be ordained, instituted or licensed, in the presence of the said bishop or his commissary, and in the form following:

I, A B do swear by almighty God that I will pay true and canonical obedience to the Lord Bishop of C and his successors in all things lawful and honest: So help me God.

C15 OF THE DECLARATION OF ASSENT

1 (1) The Declaration of Assent to be made under this Canon shall be in the form set out below:

PREFACE
The Church of England is part of the One, Holy, Catholic and Apostolic Church worshipping the one true God, Father, Son, and Holy Spirit. It professes the faith uniquely revealed in the Holy Scriptures and set forth in the catholic creeds, which faith the Church is called upon to proclaim afresh in each generation. Led by the Holy Spirit, it has borne witness to Christian truth in its historic formularies, the Thirty-nine Articles of Religion, the Book of Common Prayer and the Ordering of Bishops, Priests and Deacons. In the declaration you are about to make will you affirm your loyalty to this inheritance of faith as your inspiration and guidance under God in bringing the grace and truth of Christ to this generation and making Him known to those in your care?

DECLARATION OF ASSENT
I, A B, do so affirm, and accordingly declare my belief in the faith which is revealed in the Holy Scriptures, and set forth in the catholic creeds and to which the historic formularies of the Church of England bear witness; and in public prayer and administration of the sacraments, I will use only the forms of service which are authorised or allowed by Canon.

(2) The preface which precedes the Declaration of Assent in the form set out above (with in each case such adaptations as are appropriate) shall be spoken by the archbishop or bishop or commissary in whose presence the Declaration is to be made in accordance with the following provisions of this paragraph and shall be spoken by him before the making of the Declaration.

(3) Every person who is to be consecrated bishop or suffragan bishop shall on the occasion of his consecration publicly and openly make the Declaration of Assent in the presence of the archbishop by whom he is to be consecrated and of the congregation there assembled.

(4) Every person who is to ordained priest or deacon shall before ordination make and subscribe the Declaration of Assent in the presence of the archbishop or bishop by whom he is to be ordained.

(5) Every person who is to be instituted or admitted to any benefice or other ecclesiastical preferment or licenced to any lectureship or preachership shall first make and subscribe the Declaration of Assent in the presence of the bishop by whom he is to be instituted or licensed or of the bishop's commissary.

(6) Every person who is to be licensed to any curacy shall first make and subscribe the Declaration of Assent in the presence of the bishop by whom he is to be licensed or of the bishop's commissary, unless he has been ordained the same day and has made the Declaration.

2. Every archbishop and bishop shall, on the occasion of his enthronement in

the cathedral church of his province or diocese, as the case may be, and before he is enthroned, publicly and openly make the Declaration of Assent in the presence of the congregation there assembled.

Before the archbishop or bishop makes the Declaration the preface which precedes the Declaration in the form set out in paragraph 1 (1) of this Canon (with the appropriate adaptations) shall be spoken by the dean or provost or, if the dean or provost is absent abroad or incapacitated through illness or the office of dean or provost is vacant, by such one of the residentiary canons as those canons may select.

3. A suffragan bishop who is to be invested by the archbishop of the province in which he is to serve shall on the occasion of his investiture publicly and openly make the Declaration of Assent in the presence of the congregation there assembled.

    Before the bishop makes the Declaration, the preface which precedes the Declaration in the form set out in paragraph 1 (1) of this Canon (with the appropriate adaptations) shall be spoken by the archbishop.

4. Every minister licensed to a stipendiary curacy shall:
    (a) on the first Lord's Day on which he officiates in the church or one of the churches in which he is licensed to serve; or
    (b) in the case of a minister licensed to a stipendiary curacy in a guild church, in that church on such weekdays as the bishop may approve,

    publicly and openly make the Declaration of Assent at the time of divine service in the presence of the congregation there assembled.

    Before the minister makes the Declaration the preface which precedes the Declaration in the form set out in paragraph 1 (1) of this Canon (with the appropriate adaptations) shall be spoken by the incumbent or another priest having a cure of souls.

5. Any person who in pursuance of a request and commission from a bishop of any diocese in England is ordained by an overseas bishop within the meaning of the Overseas and Other Clergy (Ministry and Ordination) Measure 1967, or a bishop in a church not in communion with the Church of England whose orders are recognised or accepted by the Church of England shall be deemed to be ordained by a bishop of a diocese in England and accordingly shall make the Declaration of Assent.

APPENDIX II
Evangelical Patronage Societies

CPAS administers patronage for three Trusts (over 500 livings), and for the Evangelical Patronage Consultative Council keeps a Register of Clergy looking for an incumbency. All vacancies of benefices are advertised in the Archbishops'

Clergy Appointments Adviser's Vacancies List. Clergy who come on the EPCC Register (or their own CPAS Clearing House list) are met by the Patronage Secretary or one of the CPAS Trustees. When the Patronage Secretary hears of a vacancy in one of their livings, the Bishop is immediately approached for permission to move ahead in the usual way (in case a Suspension is pending). Advertisements may be placed if a parish requests it. A short list is drawn up by the trustees, after which the Bishop's clearance is sought to approach the short-listed candidates. The Trustees meet every six weeks. (A Trustee would absent him/herself from considering presenting him/herself). A P.C.C. can opt to receive 1 person at a time, or three people on different days. When the parish representatives are happy, they inform CPAS who send the name to the Bishop for his approval. The current PS has never known a nominee to be turned down by a Bishop (he has already given his clearance earlier in the procedure).

Further information can be obtained from: Patronage Secretary, Church Pastoral Aid Society, Athena Drive, Tachbrook Park, Warwick CV34 6NG, Tel: 01926 334242

Simeon's Trustees and **Hyndman Trustees** (around 150) make a list of names, some coming from the Bishop, some from Trustees, some from the EPCC Register. When they have a list of 8 or 9 names the Trustees list them in the order with which they will approach them individually. Unless the parish specifically requests it, no advertisements are placed. The Secretary can never remember a nomination being refused, because it could only happen on moral or heretical grounds.

Church Society (around 100) approaches the bishop when the parish representatives have confirmed that the person interviewed by them is acceptable. Only one person is considered at the interview stage. The bishop has thirty days to respond to that confirmation by the parish and appointment by the patrons. In the last four years a nomination was once refused, but on reasonable grounds that the Society was not in a position to know. If a Trustee is being considered for a living, he resigns from the Patronage Trust. He may be invited to take up Trusteeship again after a period of time, whether or not he was appointed.

Further information can be obtained from The Patronage Secretary, Church Society for Bible, Church and Nation, Dean Wace House, 16 Rosslyn Road, Watford, Herts WD1 7EY, Tel: 01923 235111.

Peache Trust and **Church Patronage Trust** (around 150) confer with the bishop soon after the vacancy is announced. The vacancy is advertised and a day of interviews is planned in the parish. The bishop, 2 Trustees and the parish representatives take part in the interviews. From those who have responded to the advertisements a short-list is drawn up by the Trustees, and these three or four are interviewed on the day. If a common mind is found, then one of the applicants may be offered the nomination. As the bishop has been involved refusal of licences does not arise.

APPENDIX III
The Ordination of Women to the Priesthood

Instructions for PCC's

1. Following Royal Assent for the Priests (Ordination of Women) Measure, it is expected that the Canon to make it possible for women to be ordained to the priesthood will be promulgated by the General Synod on 22nd February 1994.

Resolutions under the Measure

2. Parishes wishing to do so will be in a position to consider, and if thought appropriate, pass, the resolutions set out in Annex A (p.7) as from 1 February 1994, the date when the Measure comes into force. One never knows when a vacancy may occur (even clergy fall under buses!) and therefore it is wise for any parish which has reservations about the ordained ministry of women to consider passing Resolutions A or B

3. Any member of the PCC may ask for either or both of the resolutions in Annex A to be placed on the agenda of the PCC. The Secretary of the PCC has to give members at least 4 weeks notice of the time and place of the meeting at which the resolution or resolutions are to be considered.

4. Where the Chairman of the PCC refuses or neglects to convene a meeting to consider the resolutions, not less than one third of the members of the PCC may sign a requisition requiring him/her to call a meeting. If he/she still refuses or neglects to do so those members may forthwith convene the meeting (Church Representation Rules, Appendix 11 para. 3)

5. The PCC meeting must be attended by at least half of the members of the PCC entitled to attend. If either or both of the resolutions in Annex A is passed, a copy shall be sent to:

   a) the diocesan bishop
   b) the rural dean
   c) the lay chairman of the deanery synod
   d) the designated officer under the Patronage (Benefices) Measure 1986 (the registrar)
   e) the registered patron of the benefice

   Only a simple majority (ie more than half of the members of the PCC present and voting) is necessary to pass either of the resolutions. Ex officio and co-opted members of the PCC are full voting members.

6. Provide the above conditions are satisfied a resolution may be passed at any time after the Measure comes into force. There is no time limit either

on passing the resolution or keeping it in force. Similarly a resolution may be rescinded by the PCC at any time and the persons referred to in paragraph 5 must be notified.

7. Resolution A in Annex A cannot be considered by a PCC if the incumbent, priest-in-charge, any team vicar or assistant curate of that benefice is a woman priest.* Resolution B, which would allow a woman curate to serve in the parish but not a woman incumbent, can be considered where a women priest is serving.

    *Note: Where a woman has been ordained abroad, but is currently serving in an English parish as a deacon under the Overseas Clergy Measure 1967, she is not to be counted as a woman priest for the purpose of the Women Priests legislation whilst serving as a deacon.

District Church Councils and Conventional Districts

8. A district church council cannot pass the resolutions; they must be dealt with by the PCC although the PCC should be sensitive to any expression of opinion of a district church council. A conventional district is considered to be a parish for the purposes of the Measure and can consider the resolutions.

Team Councils, Groups and Joint Councils

9. In the case of team and group ministries and benefices held in plurality the resolutions set out in Annex A must be considered by the constituent PCC's. Thus, a PCC cannot delegate its functions under the Measure to a team council (in a team ministry) or to a group council (in a group ministry) or to a joint PCC (in a benefice with two or more separate parishes or in benefices held in plurality.

Petition for Episcopal Duties According to the Act of Synod

10. Where a PCC has passed either or both of the resolutions set out in Annex A, the members of the PCC may consider passing a further resolution to petition the diocesan bishop asking that appropriate episcopal duties should be carried out in accordance with the Episcopal Ministry Act of Synod 1993.

11. Before considering whether to petition the diocesan bishop, a PCC will need to consult widely within the parish. The advice of the PEV may be sought in connection with the making or consideration of any such petition. Views on the desirability of making a petition may differ widely and the Council will need to be sensitive to the difficulties which may arise for individuals. Especial sensitivity will be required where a parish is part of a larger unit or contains within itself several churches.

12. The terms of the resolution are not statutory but a suitable form of words is suggested in Annex B to this section. As with the resolutions in Annex A, the Secretary of the PCC must give the members at least four weeks' notice of the time and place of the meeting at which the motion is to be considered. The meeting must be attended by at least one half of the members of the PCC.

13. If the PCC passes the resolution in Annex B it should inform the diocesan bishop, the rural dean and lay chair of the deanery synod. The bishop is not obliged to make arrangements for episcopal duties to be carried out in the parish in accordance with the act of Synod unless at least two-thirds of the members of the PCC present and voting are in favour of the resolution. However, if the PCC passes the resolution by a simple majority but a two-thirds majority was not achieved or the incumbent or priest in charge is not in favour of the resolution, the bishop may still make arrangements if he considers it expedient to do so.

14. Where a resolution under the Act of Synod is in force in the parish the PCC is required to review the working of any arrangements at least once in every period of five years. If the PCC decides to withdraw a petition this should be done subject to the same conditions as were required for the adoption of a petition (see paragraph 12 above).

Annex A
Forms of Parish Resolution under the Priests (Ordination of Women) Measure 1993

Resolution A
That this parochial church council would not accept a woman as the minister who presides at or celebrates the Holy Communion or pronounces the Absolution in the parish.

Resolution B
That this parochial church council would not accept a woman as the incumbent or priest-in-charge of the benefice or as a team vicar for the benefice.

Annex B
Forms of Parish Resolution under the Episcopal Ministry Act of Synod 1993

This parochial council resolves to petition the diocesan bishop requesting that appropriate episcopal duties in the parish should be carried out in accordance with the Episcopal Ministry Act of Synod 1993.

The pitfalls of making an appointment are many. One churchwarden who has been through the process gives us the benefit of his experience, and some practical tips for getting it right .

CHAPTER 5

Appointments: a churchwarden's view

Participating in the selection of a new incumbent is possibly the most important role a churchwarden has. Our particular congregation, a large parish church with a strong evangelical tradition, underwent an interregnum in 1992/3, and these thoughts stem from my involvement as churchwarden in the appointment process. Perhaps I had a better advantage than most, having grown up in a vicarage, but the process can be quite daunting if you have no experience of interviewing or assessing people.

When an incumbent resigns, the PCC must elect two parish representatives to be involved in the selection process, and this responsibility usually falls on the churchwardens. The rest of this chapter assumes that the churchwardens are elected as parish representatives.

Churchwardens' rights

For nine months after the incumbent leaves, the churchwardens have the legal right to veto all nominations put forward by the patron or bishop, if they prayerfully consider that God's choice has not been nominated. If no appointment is made at that time, the responsibility is taken out of the patron and churchwarden's hands and reverts to the Archbishop of Canterbury.

This gives the churchwardens enormous influence over the appointment of the next incumbent, and it is vital that, once the clock has started ticking for this nine months, that you start to work hard at the job of finding a new minister. Nine months may seem like a long time, but it is not. To make a good decision, and to get the best possible candidate for the job, it is important to put in a lot of work finding out about people who may be appropriate and available. Do not leave your assessment of individuals to the interview room alone.

Prayer

It is vital that the whole appointment process is undergirded by prayer for God's choice to be made. The wardens, the PCC and the whole church need to be regularly praying. So keep them informed of progress, problems and prayer points. This undergirding of prayer – by the church, the bishop and the patrons – will keep the whole process God centred, and prevent it degenerating into a question of personal preferences.

The Nomination Process

The first job is to draft a parish profile for the PCC to give the patron. This gives details of the parish, its size, liveliness, churchmanship, and a profile of the 'ideal' incumbent.

The next task is to ensure the bishop does not suspend the living, either as part of a reorganisation or as a precursor to an amalgamation or to save money or to increase his influence over the conduct of his diocesan clergy. Archdeacons and area deans often advise the bishop on these matters. It helps enormously, therefore, if the churchwardens have *already* got to know their bishop, archdeacon and area deans before the appointment process has begun.

Patrons

Every church has a patron whose job it is to, in theory, to manage the appointment process on behalf of the church. There are three distinct types:

1. The amateur. The job of patron can be handed down from individual to individual in people's wills. This often leads to bizarre circumstances, where the patron may not be a professing Christian, or even a churchgoer. I met one patron who advised me to advertise for a new vicar in *Horse & Hounds*, as it produces the right type of candidate!

2. The patronage trust. Fortunately, many of our predecessors donated their patronage to trusts which are professional, well organised and seeking God's will for the vacancy. However, in practice, they cannot know the parish's needs as well as the churchwardens. Also, they are concerned to assist clergy who wish to move. As with all important jobs, the best person —and God's person—for a vacancy may not yet know that they wish to move.

3. Bishops. Many bishops are excellent patrons, but they can have the same weaknesses as patronage trusts. In addition, they can have hidden agendas of promoting their own churchmanship: *caveat emptor* — let the buyer beware!

After writing the parish profile and speaking with the bishop to ensure that the living is not suspended or amalgamated, the churchwardens should meet with the patrons and encourage them to advertise the vacancy as widely as possible, and to opt for the 'three at a time' shortlist method. In my opinion, shortlisting one person at a time can waste a lot of time, and gives insufficient opportunity to compare candidates. You should also consider an advertising campaign of your own, perhaps in journals or magazines that reflect your particular theological stance, to supplement that of the patron.

Go Headhunting!

The most important thing to do at this stage, however, is to get proactive: to seek out suitable candidates and encourage them to reply to the adverts. No-one knows the needs of the parish better than the churchwardens and the local church members. Churchwardens should 'get on their bikes', talk to former curates and incumbents, and to anyone else who is connected into a network of clergy, for names of possible candidates, and then go and visit these potential candidates on their home ground.

There are few appointments in the secular world where it is possible to find out so much about a potential candidate without them knowing about it. Over a three-month period, I visited 17 churches at their morning services *incognito*. I heard the vicar preach; I saw how his church greeted newcomers; I collected the parish literature; sampled a service; asked people what they thought of their minister; and generally got a feel for the man, his style and his ministry in a way that would be impossible by just listening to tapes or interviewing.

Having selected our own shortlist, we wrote to six vicars enclosing the parish profile and asking if they would consider whether God was calling them to our church and whether we could visit them to discuss and pray about it.

The selection process

Once the wardens have got their preferred candidates to apply to the patron, the rest is easy. If the patrons have any sense, they will meet with the wardens and work out together a shortlist to offer the bishop. Of course, it is also possible that one of bishop's or patron's candidates is God's person for the job, so humility is also required.

The wardens, and perhaps two other people, should form an interviewing panel. It is vital that at least two of the panel have visited each candidate's church, attended a service and heard the candidate preach.

We allowed half a day to show the candidates, and their wives, around the parish, to share a meal, and to have an hour or two of formal interview and prayer together.

The appointment

When the churchwardens have made their decision, they should indicate to the patron their veto of the other candidates. The patron is not obliged to make the preferred appointment, but cannot appoint those who have been vetoed.

In practice, if you, as wardens, show sufficient determination and application to the job of finding a suitable person, it is unlikely that you will be opposed by either patrons or bishop. However, another note of caution: patrons and bishops are often good judges of men, and their advice may well be worth listening to with humility.

One responsibility that many congregations and lay people fail in is to adequately look after their minister. Especially after a long interregnum, when people are exhausted, lay folk are only too keen to drop everything and 'let the professional get on with it.' This not only displays a woeful misunderstanding of the nature of church, but often hampers the real work of the pastor, and sometimes crushes him under the load. Traditionally, the bishop is seen as the pastor to the pastors, but he is rarely the most available or the best person for the job.

CHAPTER 6

Who pastors your pastor?

In any church, the minister of the Gospel also needs to receive the ministry of the Gospel. Like the rest of the congregation, he is sinful and in need of encouragement and rebuke. He needs to grow in holiness.

We neglect the spiritual care of the pastor to our cost. A spiritually bankrupt pastor has no resources with which to do his job—the job of encouraging and leading his flock.

But whose responsibility is it? Who should pastor your pastor?

Incidentally, throughout this chapter, we will use the word 'pastor' to refer to the person placed in charge of a congregation—the minister, rector, vicar or whatever else you might call him.

Unbiblical Responses

There are two wrong responses to the problem: one is to rely on other 'professional' pastors for encouragement; the other is to rely on denominational officials.

Depending on other pastors to encourage your pastor creates an elite class that is inconsistent with Scripture. Of course, it is natural that people who have trained for the ministry together or who have been associated in some way in the past, should turn to each other for advice and encouragement. But for a congregation to unload the spiritual care of their pastor onto his fellow professionals is extremely unwise. It places him in a different class, as if something more substantial than the application of the Word of God to his life is required. If the pastor does not confess his sins to, and receive encouragement from, his 'laymen', an unbiblical hierarchy is created.

Building this hierarchy along denominational lines is even more unbiblical. Moderators and presidents and bishops are not in the New Testament at all! If we give the denominational officials the job of 'ministering to the minister', we not only set up a pattern that is quite foreign to the New Testament, but we are left with a further unresolved question—who ministers to the bishops? If you say, "Cardinals", you are only a short step away from having a pope. If you say, "other bishops", you have fallen into the error in the previous paragraph.

To think that denominational officials will meet the spiritual needs of pastors is not only unbiblical—it is impractical as well. In most denominations there are far too few officials to even begin to do the job. And it would cost us far too much to employ extra people to do it. The average pastor can look after a congregation of about 150. He speaks to them all at least once each week (during the church meeting) and catches up with all of them personally at regular intervals. He can share informal times with them, get to know them, and be in a position to offer encouragement and fellowship.

A denominational official , sitting in an office in the city, has no hope of conducting this sort of ministry to the ministers allegedly in his care. There are few opportunities to meet together, and even fewer chances for informal chats.

Both of these responses fail to take account of some significant New Testament themes: the priesthood of all believers, our equal standing before God, our equal humility before the Word, and our equal partnership in ministry. The congregation must minister to itself. One or two members of that congregation may be freed from normal employment to work full-time to serve the members but they never cease to be members of the congregation, which is the Body of Christ. The church members must love and serve each other. Why should one or two members be exempt?

Whatever associations we might have outside our churches, and whatever encouragement or help we might receive from these, the focus of our ministry should be our church.

So who pastors the pastor?

"Confess your sins to one another" says James in the fifth chapter of his letter, and it is an old Protestant joke to say, "But we can't find the Rev. One Another anywhere!".

All the same it is sad that we have forgotten our Protestant heritage and no longer regard the pastor as being as much in need of rebuke and encouragement as the rest of us. We have lost sight of the New Testament model of mutual ministry. "Brothers, if someone is caught in a sin, you who are spiritual should restore him gently. But watch yourself, or you also may be tempted. Carry each other's burdens, and in this way you will fulfil the law of Christ" (Gal. 6:1-2).

The congregation should pastor their pastor. This is not only in keeping with the emphasis of the New Testament but is far more practical. The congregation is in the best position to care for their pastor. In the web of personal relationships between a pastor and the members of his congregation, there is ample opportunity for sharing spiritual things, for encouragement and for rebuke. The congregation will be aware of their pastor's shortcomings and will be able to help him through them in a way that no outsider could.

If the pastor is not open to receive this ministry from his congregation, they will also tend to be closed to his ministry to them. A pastor who is open with his congregation and who is ready to expose his weakness and receive care, will encourage the same attitude among his congregation. As in all things, the pastor serves as a model. If he is self-sufficient and seemingly beyond the need for normal fellowship and encouragement, then that is the goal towards which his congregation will strive. They will try to become as self-sufficient and closed as their pastor.

It is worth noting the words Paul uses with his junior pastor, Timothy. "Be diligent in these matters; give yourself wholly to them, so that everyone may see your progress." The pastor is not required to have 'arrived'. Like all Christians, he is on a journey, and like all Christians, he is required to make progress. The pastor who gives the impression that he has 'arrived' is a discouragement for Christian growth. He might think that he is providing a godly model, but he is actually providing a very unhelpful model, one that is open to the charge of hypocrisy. He must model godly progress. He must listen to the Word of God, take it to heart and change his life. This is the model for the congregation to follow.

Obstacles

We have already hinted that the pastor himself can prevent his own spiritual nurture. Too many pastors lock themselves away, spiritually speaking, by being unable or unwilling to receive the ministry of others. Many pastors are used to switching into 'ministry mode' whenever they are with members of their congregation. They feel so responsible for everyone else that they lose the ability to talk to their people as equals and receive help from them.

Those who carry the Word of God to others can easily fall into the trap of always teaching it, but never listening to it. It is not even enough for the pastor to apply the Word privately as he prepares his sermon. He must be ready to do so publicly as he interacts with members of the congregation, and to listen to God's word no matter who is speaking it—for "from the lips of children ad infants you have ordained praise" (Ps. 8:2).

Many pastors find it almost impossible to receive the ministry of others because their own insecurity. They may be unsure about their role or their ability to carry it out, and they become defensive. The pastor may feel that if he reveals too much of himself, he may be seen as a weak leader, and lose control. As a result, he holds it all in and discourages others from taking the initiative. The pastor caught in this trap will rarely be aware of the spiritual corner into which he has painted himself.

Pastors are encouraged along this path by the whinging and criticism that they so often bear. Everybody knows how to run the church, and the constant griping ends to drive the pastor back into his shell. He protects himself by refraining from any kind of interaction at this level.

Another problem for the pastor is the sheer number of people who might minister to him. He is known by all, and his foibles and shortcomings are seen by all, and members usually feel they have the right to comment on them—mostly to each other, but sometimes to the pastor himself.

Finally, the pastor can also fall victim to the tyrannous expectations of church life. Many of these expectations are all the more impossible because they are unstated. There are many expectations that a pastor may feel he should live up to—expectations dictated by society, or his denominational tradition, or his predecessor at the church. There may be expectations about how much work he does each week, or how he runs his family, or the clothes he wears, or the cars he drives, or the hobbies he pursues.

One a pastor accepts the mantle of these expectations, and fails to meet them (as he inevitably will) he begins to hid. His guilt becomes a barrier between him ad his congregation. He will not open up to them and allow them to minister to him, for fear that they will see his 'double life'.

Congregations, for their part, are frequently reluctant to approach the pastor to help him in his walk with God. To a certain extent, this reluctance is born out of an appropriate reverence for those who have been placed over us in the Lord.

However, it is more usually the result of an inappropriate elevation of the pastor onto some super-spiritual pedestal. Many congregations regard their pastor as a breed apart, rather than as a fellow heir of the kingdom, who is as much in need of care and spiritual nurture as all of us.

A further problem is that many congregations have swallowed an hierarchical, institutional view of ministry, and so leave the care of the pastor to the bishops and moderators of the denomination. It is sad that we Evangelicals, who like to affirm the priesthood of all believers and the importance of ever-member ministry, have sold our birthright on this issue. We need to return to our roots. But perhaps the chief reason for congregations failing to pastor their pastors is that they don't know how. Even if the congregation is willing and the pastor is open, it is still hard to work out how to do it effectively. Her are some clues:

1. **Not everyone must do the same thing all at once.** If a pastor has a particular fault, the last thing he needs is for the whole congregation, one by one, to take him aside and tell him in earnest tones about his need to repent. The congregation needs to be sensitive, and to ensure that someone is ministering to the pastor on this point, without him being overwhelmed. Those who exercise leadership within the congregation—the elders, deacons, church wardens, or whatever, must surely be the ones to see that this happens.

2. **We shouldn't define ministry too narrowly.** While pastors do need to receive personal encouragement about their spiritual lives, there are other kinds of ministry that can be just as helpful. The warm greeting, the short letter, prayerful support, the gift of food, baby-sitting, a phone call on his birthday—there are many things that a congregation can do to encourage and help the pastor in his task. Unfortunately, these small, casual encouragements can go unnoticed, both by the pastor when he feels that no-one cares for him, and by the congregation when they feel guilty at their lack of care.

   Pastoring the pastor does not necessarily mean having deep and meaningful conversations with him. There is a time for this, just as there is in relationships among congregation members but this is not the norm. Informally sharing a passage of Scripture that we have found helpful, or asking questions about some aspect of the sermon, or sharing a book with him that we have found beneficial—there are endless ways we can pastor the pastor.

3. **We do not always have to be negative.** There is a time for discussing problems and sins, and for rebuking and correcting. But there is also a time for encouragement, and congratulation, and positive feedback. Pastors find tremendous encouragement in seeing their people grown in understanding and holiness. To share

with him ways in which this is happening is a great ministry to him—it spurs him on in the arduous work of the Gospel.

When he does something helpful or encouraging, we should not hold back in telling him so. The polite "Good sermon this morning" does some good, but is fairly conventional and almost mandatory. To mention a particular point of the sermon and how you found it helpful will do any preacher's heart good.

4. **We must minister in relationship over time.** Serving and caring for our pastors takes time. It is important that we develop a relationship with our pastor that God can use for mutual encouragement over time. It will not be possible for every member to have this relationship, especially in a large congregation, but the members of the church committee, at the very least, should have some ongoing relationship with the pastor. As we develop this relationship, we will have the opportunity of speaking the quiet word of encouragement and rebuke.

5. **We need to listen as well as speak.** Pastors need someone to listen to the troubles that inevitably accompany Gospel ministry. The person who can listen and understand the pastor's struggles will be the one who can offer a genuine and timely word of encouragement in the future. This person will also, no doubt, be the one to whom the pastor turns in times of personal trouble. He or she will also be the one who can enquire about the pastor's personal life. Pastor's cannot cope with every member of the congregation asking him about his quiet times. It soon becomes a tedious, not to say legalistic, charade. However, most pastors are never asked about their quiet times.

If the pastor can develop this kind of empathetic relationship with one or two or five or ten members of his congregation, there will be ample opportunity over time for the pastor to be pastored.

An urgent need

For too many pastors, the work of the Gospel is a lonely and frustrating battle. They feel isolated and unloved, and become resentful of their congregation, who are quick to return the favour by grumbling and counting the years until he retires.

Spending time pastoring the pastor is a valuable investment. The congregation, and particularly he congregation's leaders, must take responsibility for the spiritual health and vitality of their own pastor. We must not leave it to other pastors or to distant denominational officials, but prayerfully should bear the responsibility ourselves.

CONTRIBUTORS

Hugh Balfour is vicar of Christ Church Old Kent Road, and is chairman of Reform Southwark

John Richardson—formerly chaplain at the University of East London—is now Assistant Minister in the United Benefice of Henham, Elsenham and Ugley.

Jonathan Fletcher is incumbent of Emmanuel Church, Wimbledon.

Phillip Jensen is rector of St Matthias Church, Centennial Park, Sydney, and chaplain at the University of New South Wales

Jonathan Thornton is churchwarden at St James, Muswell Hill

Robin Cooper is a partner with lawyers Brown Cooper, and a lay leader at Emmanuel Dundonald Church, Wimbledon.

Further information on Reform can be
obtained from:

The Reform Office
Christ Church, Fulwood,
Canterbury Avenue,
Sheffield S10 3RT.
Tel: 0114 230 1911
Fax: 0114 230 6568